okay okay okay

POEMS BY
TODD REGOULINSKY

for
Kim & Kaelin,
of course.

But,
also for
Gabe & Bill.

CONTENTS

introduction   1

ONE

on line   9

i'm going away tonight   10

i hope so   11

don't lift me   12

i won't be long   14

i'm the problem   15

suppose, suppose   16

fall(fell)ing   18

address service requested   19

how can i ever forget them   20

barrel proof   22

par accident, excusez-moi   23

surprise me   24

atmospheres   25

thrust   26

don't   27

the novice   28

all the flowers   31

TWO

give me coffee, i'm going to write   35

wonder-full   36

tendered   37

stage directions   38

nocturne   40

the score   41

love in the afternoon   42

here   44

-ectomy   45

never drive at night   47

puzzle boxes   49

it's very beautiful out there   50

delays   52

calculations   53

brace!   54

advice to my daughter   55

remember the tune?   56

in case   57

acknowledgment   59

flywheel   61

THREE

parade ground   65

the electrons between us   66

i know not what tomorrow will bring   67

so here it is: 69

i wish i could go with you   71

travel abroad, see the world!   72

maybe   74

this   76

i go to see a great perhaps   77

dionysus   78

currency   79

she spoke   80

the big lie   81

mantra   82

insomnia requiem   83

sustain   85

cool waters   86

one last drink, please   87

back in no time   88

you be good. see you tomorrow. i love you.   90

index of quotes   93

INTRODUCTION

I wrote these poems because there apparently wasn't a way that I couldn't not write them.

Yeah, kind of confusing. Let me explain.

I've been writing poetry since high school, with most of it being what I'd call confessional poems - mostly about myself, inner thoughts, feelings, and other inward-facing stuff. But that gets boring after awhile (both to write and read), and I wanted a new challenge.

Writing prompts have never been my thing because it seems a lot of them are very generic. There are some good ones, but most feel like some variation on "write a poem based on three things on your desk" or "write a poem about a color", etc. Apparently, to write a book of prompts, one starts to look around whatever space they're in and pick out whatever is handy. Which is mostly what I've done all my life, but with less book sales.

Late one night, I found myself reading a list of people's last words - what they had spoken just before dying. Yeah, not the most uplifting way to spend an evening, but it does pass the time. And it did give me an idea. What about using them as prompts or inspirations for poems? For some reason, it sounded like a good idea and I started in on it.

Shocking to almost nobody, hanging around and thinking about people's last moments before shuffling off the mortal coil is a bit morbid and there was no way to keep at it while also maintaining any kind of mental health. So I shelved it, figuring that was that. But for some reason, this idea kept coming back to me - it just wouldn't go away. I tried a couple more times, but the same thing happened - I'd lose all energy because it was a meditation on death. Who would've guessed, right?

Coming back to it again one day, I finally hit on an idea. I'd go through my collection of last words and write down only the quote on an index card - no attribution. Then, I'd shuffle the cards and leave them for a bit, not going back to the main list. After a few days, I started drawing out cards. Sometimes, the poem would come to me immediately. Other times, I had to read the card over and over. A few times, the card went back into the deck and I'd take another one.

What this did was to separate the words from their context. Being free from who said them and the baggage of who that person was freed me to make whatever connections that came to mind. Sometimes, I'd remember who'd said what, so the separation wasn't complete and some of the baggage seeped through; although I'd argue it was usually an overnight bag or shaving kit rather than a steamer trunk.

At any rate, that is how this book came about. To me, it isn't a book about death so much as a book about life finding its way through the cracks in spite of our best efforts. This idea wouldn't die for me and left me no choices but write or go nuts trying to ignore it. Which, in a way, is the way I've approached life, love, and poetry for the past forty six years.

Todd Regoulinsky
Saco, Maine - 2023

"Okay.
Okay.
Okay."

- last words of
Sam Kinnison

stand-up comedian &
scream of a generation

okay

ONE

ON LINE

traveling through this place,
we are running on line
north & south through space -

pushing beyond boundaries & walls
rubbing against eternity & falls

misjudging our steps
mistiming our jumps
farther than we've yet crept
holding to earth & sky by clumps

hoping for some grand skyward gleam
hope beyond any reason or scheme,

traveling through this place,
we are running on line
north & south through space.

I'M GOING AWAY TONIGHT

      i whispered
to the sky of my hometown -
to no one in particular
      & all those i'd known
my whole life between
a few degrees
      of latitude & longitude -

a few degrees
      state of mind and of union
unsure of destination & duration,
      staring down a broken
yellow line headed in one of four
cardinal directions
      and not caring which one -

going away from this junkyard
where the wrecks of my life
      lay stacked under frost,
unsure of future but ticket confirmed:
going away from faces & spaces
      into something (anything) else,

the "else" being most important
on this night - coffee & music
      at the ready.

"i'm going away tonight:
      i whispered
to no reply.

I HOPE SO

ghosts walk past broken windows,
hearts still, examining rocks
which once bore ill intent
but now
are still.

are they at peace?
i hope so.

my good intentions wait in line,
guillotine in shadow,
dusk creeping up on us all,
her heart
still.

is she happier now?
i hope so.

a species doomed by success
& survival, stories etched
in dust & blood, line by line
marching our way
to Hell

are we really alive?
i hope so.

DON'T LIFT ME

don't let me feel hope

don't let me feel
for one moment
a ray of sunshine through
the cracks & crags
of debris that has piled up
on top of me -

don't lift me

don't dig for me

it's too late, i whisper
through parched, dusty lips
to my would-be rescuer -
leave me be & dig for someone else
who might have a chance of survival
in the world.

don't lift me

i may crack
i may fall

don't lift me

yet the digging continues,
moving chunks of concrete & rebar
that have been guarding my tomb
for years

don't they know that if all this wreckage
is gone that i'll be nothing?

don't lift me

leave me be

but the shovels still come.

I WON'T BE LONG

we have all had
    those moments
haven't we?

    earth leaves sky,
the mind rips & tears -
    nothing makes sense
except a quick fade out
    & a tastefully lettered "The End".

we all have glanced
    at the edge
out the corner of an eye,
    but you…
you stared it down
    & paid the price.
leaving us to wonder -

    we have all
had those moments
    haven't we?

for Gabe

I'M THE PROBLEM

staring into the sun, it stares back without judgement - only
glare & spots & burning

diving into the sea, it closes over my head, breathing in - only
salt & oxygen too wet to breath

i'm the problem.

standing in the school, the bullet bites into my flesh - only
blood & burning & tearing

standing in the street, the baton thuds at my skull - only
flashes & cracking & blackness

i'm the problem.

SUPPOSE, SUPPOSE

as the sun goes, so does the moon
as the gun goes, so does the bullet -
along corridors, the dead smile
because there is nothing more
for them to worry over.

suppose, suppose.

as love goes, so does lust
as lust goes, so do lies -
pillows tell the truth,
all their observations,
bearing witness to dreams
& sins in silence.

suppose, suppose.

as the earth goes, so does sky
as the sky goes, so does night -
confusion wear false glasses
& mustache to stroll in public
while buildings cautiously watch
for stray matches.

suppose, suppose
that this world is all it is
because of you and i,
that it is all it ever will be.

suppose, suppose
that it is more beautiful
than we'll ever know.

FALL(FELL)ING

the second time we made love,
she whispered: "please don't let me fall" -

one year later,
she was in someone else's arms
& i suppose she fell
after all.

my question is still:
did i drop her
or
did she jump?

ADDRESS SERVICE REQUESTED

hastily-taped cardboard boxes
full of years,
clothes bearing her scent, and
mixtapes -
with erased
& re-recorded songs
i no longer recognized.

comforting myself with cracked thoughts:
       all things end
       life goes on
       other fish in the sea
       darkest before the dawn.

but saying:
       i expected
       it to happen

doesn't change
the change of address card
in my back pocket,
does it?

HOW CAN I EVER
FORGET THEM

there's a tattoo of my name
on her right inner thigh,
approximately an inch & three quarters
from…
well…
you know.

simple letters defying the intricacy
of two hearts
tied together -
intersecting lines represent veins
& arteries which once
carried something like love
(but maybe not quite)

      my apologies for equivocating, but
      past loves are cloudy as ancient wars:
      blurred battlefields, sabotage &
      subterfuge. countless mass graves -

      casualties unto themselves
      & the truth itself.

let us just say there was love,
however fleeting or faint,
shall we?

memorialized in underskin ink
are kisses, laughter,
promises kept & broken,
the supernova in her eyes
when i opened the door,
& glazed recognition
when it closed

a series of once-upon-a-times
edited for broadcast length,
but we're still there
somewhere
in those lines,
ghosts of ourselves
not so much haunting as haunted -
by failed potential,
time & human nature
no matter how deserved &
faultless they might have been.

that spot, kissed & loved
as the rest of her,
now memorialized in ink
of two kinds now
with even more questions created

when some new lover
points & asks:
"so who were they?"

BARREL PROOF

you know how it goes seeing ghosts:
old lovers as shadows
refusing exorcism

codeine… bourbon… the only words i can sing
one last gasp & these are a few of my favorite things.

self-medication by self-deprecation is the only self-defense
in this era of errors & easy offense - chiming over & over
but i guess the jokes on me because i'm a fighter not a lover.

codeine… bourbon… if only i could get a little taste
& check your back pocket for your wallet just in case.

& if this seems a little strong to bear, some medicine
that no sugar accompanies - perhaps you should change
the company you keep and prepare for that faithful leap -

codeine… bourbon… maybe there's a little more left
hotwiring my heart for getaway in case of grand theft.

blinders on my eyes & heart is the only solution, but
a saltwater tear dilution is the only trick i've ever known…
no matter what i've been shown

codeine… bourbon… balancing between one world & another
broken apart is the only way we've ever been good together.

PAR ACCIDENT, EXCUSEZ-MOI

pardon me.
i didn't do it on purpose.

i didn't tear skyholes
in earth or
dig dusty clouds
in sunset -
nor tidal waves of sound
nor avalanche of roses
to arrive on your doorstep.

this business of love
is darts in darkness,
the merest chance of luck -
a breath when drowning.

perhaps an
unfortunate what
of the kind which
i don't know - a tell
that will not reveal
its secrets,

       it was this:
a stagger & bump of chance
into this moment,
when sideways i fell
and there, unbeknownst
to herself,
was she.

SURPRISE ME

love me

mistreat me

ignore me

nag   hector   pester me

kiss me

caress   fondle   feel me

understand me

miss me?

believe me

shelter me

melt me

shatter me

whatever you do,

surprise me.

ATMOSPHERES

outerspace turned inner
and beginning's end twisted
into pretzels full of strychnine with
delicious kosher salt crystals to cut the sting:
tragedies punctuated with punchlines
making palatable the prison.

i can't breath out here
and i can't breath in there
so the time has come
for a third option.

pushing against pressure
holding insides in and outsides out
…
or was it downs down and ups up?

it's so hard to remember these things
with a boot in the back
and a stick across a throat -
improvising the performance art of
"how to stay alive in 10 easy steps"
as the cold concrete prepares flesh
for the cold atmosphere
of a slab.

THRUST

trusty roses, dangling upsidedown
on the insideout of mind, declaring:

> this too shall pass underover
> bridges like so much water -

underthrough and overinside is
the only waypath to understanding,

> to which the reply seems
> underwhelmingly oversimplified

now comes the mystery, to be unsolveddiscovered
as we wonderwander along days constructed

> of breaths&bread, seconds&crumbs
> of each kind of life&death

turning backfront, the whispers grow faint
& we go rightsideup back through

> the deadly dandelions, searching
> for freedom&servitude.

DON'T

words set like traps:
forming lines, phrases, & paragraphs
that spin into stories masquerading
as people -
brought slowly into the chute,
down to the killing floor.

whispering to neighbors:
when they come for you,
don't look up -
don't disturb my circles!
don't give them satisfaction,
leave them wanting.

push & shove,
past & present
hold their breath,
and then … gone.

leaving behind only
a hole in the air,
wondering wheredtheygo?!

passing from one place to another,
wherewecant.

THE NOVICE

c'mon in
she said
the water is fine

      a novice approaches the altar

don't worry
it's not
loaded

      a novice approaches the altar

a hum
fills the air
between

      as a novice approaches the altar

electricity
can be felt
miles away

      as the novice approaches the altar

shocks of
recognition
are felt

      as a novice approaches the altar

& once again
lambs are
slaughtered

 as the novice approaches the altar

taken in,
loved & then
forgotten

 the novice approaches the altar

only to be
seen & heard,
then forgotten

 as another novice approaches the altar

hoping to
be something more
than the others

 the novice approaches the altar

only to be
dismissed
as a heretic

 as the novice approaches the altar

television &
satellites bear witness
to it all

      as the novice approaches the altar

& minces them-
selves into
something else

      a novice approaching the altar

becomes
something else
entirely

      once the novice approaches the altar

& is seen
for the first time
& perhaps the last

      as a novice approaching the altar.

ALL THE FLOWERS

seem to say:
you will not
find me alive at sunrise.

for all its beauty,
life is a small thing -
& barely grasped
(let alone held).

moon crosses sky,
dipping its fingers into a
nothing that is
all colors at once -

hurtling towards a nothing
while petals collect dew

until the moment they don't.

okay

TWO

GIVE ME COFFEE, I'M GOING TO WRITE

i haven't been reading enough poetry

the world seems sideways

the president of the united states is a dolt

a friend is dead

i've been drinking too much whiskey

the world doesn't make sense

politicians are educated and uneducated whores

another friend is going mad

i haven't been drinking enough whiskey

the world makes too much sense

the town council voted to legalize legality

a friend calls and needs a hundred bucks

i've given up whiskey for wine

the same politicians are up for promotion

a friend has been fired & is homeless

the world is a wildfire too beautiful for words

i'm back to whiskey & declared my love

the world doesn't love me back

the president can jump off a pier for all i care

a friend tried to lure me into her bed

whiskey doesn't love me back

the governor won't grant a pardon

my friends have turned off their phones

i haven't been reading enough poetry

have you?

WONDER-FULL

we reach out in the dark,
a doomed species
if ever there was one,
hoping for some panacea -
comforting ourselves in
purple prose & tropes such as:

"nothing soothes pain
like human touch"

maybe i missed
that meeting.

somewhere between sleep
& voluntary insomnia,
the inebriation of solitude
takes hold
& i am adrift -

& it feels
wonder-full.

TENDERED

for hearing,
we need a language:
      full of gamble &
      pierced through
      with truth -

a language tattooed
with words worthy
of being masticated,
      turned back to pulp,
      devoured & processed,
      rejected, then left -

all for another group,
generation, or a murder
of idealists,
      pecking away at
      the corn of dead
      centuries & wondering:

did they mean it?
with their lives?
feel it in their loins?
      maybe an answer
      is somewhere being
      written rightnow

more than likely not
here or where you
are either.

STAGE DIRECTIONS

enter stage right,
this dead-eyed vapor of mine,
here to deliver one single line & leave,
comic relief incarnate
 - in the flesh,
in the meat, in the pulse-and-breathing
sort of thing that always
seems to do it for the crowd.
audience expecting words of wisdom (or
perhaps some catchy phrase to exchange over
drinks & smokes late that evening), only to be
rewarded with sound & little fury - a gasp
in the general direction of eternity &
full of utter nonsense.

but at the least, this nonsense belongs to me -
not yours or the property of some conglomerate,
some focus group of minds that never left
high school. it's a nonsense that still retains
some flavor - whether it agrees with you or not.

relying on little more than wits & desperation,
the method of this performance isn't lost on me -
a one-way sort of fling with ink & paper
which is only honored in theory, not practice,
but at the very least, it's a decent way
to pass the time… even if critics
can't agree or bring themselves
to applaud the downs as well as
ups.

have i played the part well?
then applaud me as i exit.

NOCTURNE

i'll sleep well tonight,
because any dream could kill me
with their straight-edge smiles
& dynamite embrace.

this is how i'll fall into rest:
with nothingness in my eyes,
her in my heart, &
a busted smile
in my pocket.

THE SCORE

the world collapses in on itself: implosions
          of test tube lightning and parchment,
calling out to calendar pages gone by -
          ripping one day from another's arms

and i can hear the music all around me.

we represent all manner of injustice & divinity
          moving both directions at once,
going nowhere & in a hurry to get there but
          somehow maintaining our grasp on grace -

and i can hear the music all around me.

while the bombs fall, the babies cry, & the
          old men send young men off to die ;
while the world melts & reforms unconcerned
          shaking mankind off like fleas

i can hear the music all around me.

recalcitrant moments of reticence hold these
          truths evident in the light of day, mistaken
for rockets red glare: that all peoples are created
          in a dearth of vision - where those without perish,

and i can hear the music all around me.

LOVE IN THE AFTERNOON

at this point, it is necessary
that you be in love:

        if it were described to you,

        it would not be

        the love you know

        or have known.

it is necessary to accept
this mystery at face value -

        to reach escape velocity

        beyond the gravity of lust

        into the ether between worlds:

        that is love.

that is not always easy & shouldn't be,
as inescapable responsibility should -

        this dance between

        want & need, dispersing

        our own illusions

        of future & past.

to whisper " good night my kitten"
without guile or remorse -

        embracing all the drear,

        drama, & drag that comes

        with dreams & drastic

        turns of fortune.

we know what we know & nothing
of what we don't but that we don't -
            and this is best of all,
            by far.

HERE

i have found a great nothing, so here it is.
i have tended a garden, so here it is.
i have grown weary & found my grave to lie down in,
       so here it is.

no more of this stumbling & stabbing at the edges
of immortality - pretending some kind of small monument
here in the middle of a green field,
no more imagining words well-preserved in
the amber of pulpy pages to be thumbed through
at some later time.

i have found a great nothing, so here it is.
i have tended a garden that grows no more, so here it is.
i have laid down for rest & the roots have grown over me,
       so here it is.

-ECTOMY

removal of the heart
is a tricky operation
at the best of times,
& at the worst,
doubly so.

her knife was by far
the sharpest of any
i'd encountered,
& she knew exactly
how to wield it.

a turn of the wrist
which i'd kissed so often,
just a flick, really,
& the blood flowed
pure & true.

moments later, a
mere breath of ether
to dull the burn,
& it was all over
except the stitches.

surgery complete:
how do you feel
she asked?
& i replied,
i feel pain here.

that's normal,

she said.

you'll

feel better

tomorrow.

NEVER DRIVE AT NIGHT

headlights shine through me,
dirty windshields for eyes
& an overheated straight-six in my skull.

i wander over roads like
black veins pumping
me from one vital organ
to another - Boston   Baton Rogue
Boca Raton   Barstow   Big Sur   -
my oxygen: carbon monoxide
(your poison, my pleasure) -
windshield wiper symphonies
echoing through blown-out speakers.

the green of highway signs
the same & different
as currency & envy
of those rooted, contented masses
who aren't cursed/blessed to shark-like
forward movement,

amphetamine smiles & truck stop chili
are my family crest, rusted through
along the rocker panels,
still-solid frame doesn't know
any better, holds together &
moves on through the night.

there's a search somewhere, an APB,
but i've lost the scent
along with radio signal;
merge left or right,
oblivion
next 50 miles.

PUZZLE BOXES

love one
another
before
time passes
too far
& we stand
on shores,
oceans part,
calling out
names
we barely
remember
still

another
one love
goes out
through
slammed door,
a mockery
of itself
& stale
on the wind -
a memory
& nothing more
than ghosts
& salt.

IT'S VERY BEAUTIFUL OUT THERE

misshapen shadows
& will-o-wisps dance,
twisting in whirlwinds
of lies & misgivings -

poetry in motion
away from here & horizon-bound,
searching for
greener pastures & peace.

there is only war here:
on the television,
on the lips of cosplayed soldiers
who belong in asylums
& public servants who
belong in jails.

war is good for business
& morale -
economies are built on it,
modern moneychanger's eyes
roll to the backs of their heads
in ecstasy at its mere mention.

the populace never seems
to know peace - we have:
a war on drugs
a war on poverty
a war on each other
a war on immigrants
a war on immorality

but never a war on war.

but outside this window,
over there, a spot
of beauty remains
            unblemished

they haven't seen it yet
they haven't spoiled it yet.

quick,
fold it carefully
& place it in your pocket -

save it for later…

i have a feeling
you'll need it.

DELAYS

why does love walk so slowly?
moving in strides almost imperceptible to the eye -
a parody of itself and yet so holy
as to inspire silence in all
who surround it?

why does it always seem to go so quickly?
moving like a herd of bison
on range with no care of obstacles
or walls or breakable hearts & bones,
trampling ever forward?

why does she always want more ?
more without giving, moving hands
through pockets deftly
as saints with light fingers,
as demons with knives so sharp that the blade winks
before sinking into flesh for its final resting place?

why is the world so full of nothing?
bulging at the seams
with stuffing that reveals nothing & only
seems existent to slow us all down while keeping inside & out apart,
its own type of segregation without end.

why is this taking so long?

CALCULATIONS

the eye stares at the screen
& the screen stares back,
neither blink.

a scene like this one, repeated over and over throughout time & space, represents
the smallest of humanity's indulgences - the briefest of gasps given to beings big
and small. short of that thisness,
for which there is nothing there for perception to perceive or receptors to receive -
a dullness which no thusness may sharpen or polish.

the hand touches the skin
& the skin recoils,
neither move.

perhaps the best to be hoped for is a division which rejoins at some point:
of unique hearts becoming a single muscle, a single piston driving Life
through veins which becomes a kind of Love,
a sort of Type O-negative universal donor in search of its AB-positive recipient -
or are we verging into hyperbole here?

the life touches death
& eternity shudders,
neither change.

all that can be silently said at times such as this is that one without one isn't zero
but one, defying all mathematics & physics which say differently.
am i dying or is this my birthday?
the answer is, of course, both.

BRACE!

somewhere over Omaha
the American Dream flames out,
gliding through the dingy
flannel-textured clouds -
suddenly silent.

while drink carts wheel
through first class, economy
knows the drill:
feet apart, heads down!
so like a police shakedown
it'd be funny if not
for the decreasing altitude.

a makeshift runway fire is lit
in some government-subsidized corn field
as pilot cracks wise to
navigator: "hold the cross high
so that i may see it
through the flames" …

surely,
Christ help all us doomed sinners,

but for now,

brace!

ADVICE TO MY DAUGHTER

don't be in such a hurry, i say
this world will blur & fray
without any help at all -
don't push it along, lay your head
gently on pillows & shoulders,
careful of each choice.

don't be in such a hurry,
each day is its own equation -
some never balancing & others
solve themselves, but either way,
never be ashamed
to show your work.

REMEMBER THE TUNE?

days like this,
                    sunshine drips in
through windows, then   suddenly,

disperses into   a   thousandpieces -

shards of nothing
                         falling
                                 down
                                      into
                                              us.
while the rest of the world
cries or laughs, i sit & stare at spectacles
beyond measure
                         and when
          the looks
come,

i smile & say
              "go away
i'm all right"

IN CASE

in case no one else has the heart to tell you,
you are wonderful.

in case no one else has the courage to tell you,
you are amazing.

in case no one else can bring themselves to say it
because they're too busy trying to push themselves
to the top of the heap of a rusty world
that's got nothing to offer but a tetanus shot
and a kick in the head; because they've lost
all the things they once thought they wanted
& are too lazy to dream new dreams,
so they spend day & night tearing others apart;
in case they succeed in getting to you, in case
they find some crack in your armor, in case
all else fails, let me be the one to say
you are wonderful.

you are the end result of millennia upon millennia
wrestling against each other inside
the trappings of our cantankerous human experience:
you are the pearl of all this war and suffering and
laughter and dreams - made for times such as these
& granted breath for the purpose of standing alone
in this room now, wondering what comes next &
if it will lead to something greater.

don't worry, it will.

in case there's too much static on the radio tonight,
let me dictate the songs to you
on an old rusty typewriter with ten stuck keys and
a missing ampersand, titter-tatting our way towards
something akin to immortality that will come just short
but delicious nonetheless because it's with you.
in case the walls begin to scream, let me
be the one who whispers in your ear:
you are wonderful.

in case the world breaks your heart again and again
and again and then again…

let me repeat it ad infinitum until it becomes something
almost believable:
you are wonderful.

ACKNOWLEDGEMENT

do you wish to make confessions my son?
yes, but not too much.

allow me a precious few secrets to myself:
        this is the lie & deception of each dying man,
the silent request of diminishing returns
        until, day by day, our wishes become
fountains we are drowned in,
        one inch at a time.

so are you saying that we're all doomed?
yes, but not too much.

it's a small damnation
        awaiting us, a penny candy type
of mortal extrapolation that
        brings us to our knees
eventually, a terminal fascination
        with ourselves.

is there no hope for us?
yes, but not too much.

breath after breath, you'll process
        more oxygen & less comprehension -
this is your curse & the same of all
        generations before you, scrabbling
one after another for pennies as paper money
        flies past your ears.
do you have any last words, my son?
yes, but not too much.

words loved like needles love thread,
        give us this day our rotten bread -
as teeth pulled from gums & guns pulled from holsters,
        bullets molded of nouns struck by verbs
& fired, one after another, in any direction
        will eventually strike…

something?
yes, but not too much.

FLYWHEEL

i

    am   a

b

      roke

         n

piece of machine   ry.

specks of dirt & grit mashed into
waves of rotting monkey wrench gunk
that will

even   t   u   a l   l   y

bring this   th ing to a

        .

        .

        .

          halt.

when the ma

      chine is bro

                  ken…

i am

ready.

okay

THREE

PARADE GROUND

last words are for fools who haven't said enough
but my mind keeps winding itself up, torqued
to the point of singing out like cello strings from hell -
bursting with a thousand kinds of madness
that have no other place to go, swelling within me,
crashing against the shore of my breath.

each word seems like the last,
that something
could come along at any moment -
a perfect predator, ready to ascend
to its place atop the food chain,
leaving me the mangled remains
of a discarded prototype

well, on most nights, that's all right with me.

immortality & reality being relative,
not pretending to one & only playing at the other,
these words (which could be last or just next)
are my company, my friends, & tormentors -

if only typewriter ribbons were still in fashion,
i'd drape my windows in them like patriotic bunting,
a salute to my minor obsession
as the words pass in review.

THE ELECTRONS BETWEEN US

bursting forth upon pixelated screens,
radiating our Sunday best no matter the day,
we are blindingly beautiful & perfect smiles.

on the other side of the looking glass,
we are crusty-eyed & bathrobe-cloaked
on a ripped couch wondering: "does my face look strange?"

our hidden selves revealed only to those acquainted
& accidental - like an ex-lover encountered past midnight
while buying toilet paper & potato chips.

I KNOW NOT WHAT
TOMORROW WILL BRING

but you.

your eyes of discarded broken glass will be there -
a nebula of discomfort & disbelief
swirling in gravity of its own honesty,
they will be there.

heart like a locomotive, strong & decent,
ready to pull freight cars
full of wonder & horrors both known & unknown -
it will be there.

love like a worn elastic band -
used & discarded hundreds of times, yet
still holding shape -
a hope that bouncing back again & again
will be some kind of holy virtue
that will unlock immortality, or
at least get us through one more night -
that rubberband love
will be there.

these things are known:
when so many unknown carry
nothing but suitcases of fear,
these thoughts are my baggage
claimed on this sleepless night
that is mine to travel.

somehow i know,
no matter what tomorrow brings,
they too will be there.

SO HERE IT IS:

a confession by declaration,
a defamation by way of a concession -

the tide has turned up
more of pastime than time that's passed

between moments we danced around
moments, hung in the air as ripened fruit,
waiting to be plucked
and this situation waiting to be …

our love - our time

shoved in a bag & tossed into the trunk,
knocked against the spare, sunk into the nearest river
with all the other incriminating evidence

but knowing where the bodies are buried
doesn't make the bodies any less bodily,

nobody knowing that if apart, anybody
could fill that space & raise a commotion
until somebody pounded on the door to
keep it THE FUCK down IN THERE!

there is where
the problems always seemed to begin,

this means to an end was always an end unto itself,
us being nothing more than more trouble
than each being was willing to take on -

so here it is:
unable to leave, stuck between
ourselves and the rising water,
a moment only understood
by other failed escape artists,
we breathed deeply
and accepted fate

because this is more truth than either
had a right to expect, & this moment together
would keep us warm separately
for years
to come.

I WISH I COULD GO WITH YOU

on adventures & disasters,
burning wrecks along with the shining days,
to libraries among the big stacks of books
with their stories & smell of ancient paper,
along walks where thoughts run ahead…

i wish i could go with you
in all seasons & weather, holding umbrellas
and such over you, holding open doors and
shutting your eyes with a kiss each night…

i wish i could go with you
& see all the wonders of life, laughing
in time and breathing through silence

i wish i could go with you,
but there are things your old man
cannot do, so i hope you'll understand
some day.

TRAVEL ABROAD –
SEE THE WORLD!

we are bedraggled tourists,
too many miles
in the bags under our eyes -
all hopes & fears & dreams
stored insecurely
in overhead bins

dust and wind examining
passports - declared illegal peoples
among the outlaws,
shoved into waiting rooms
shaped like: apartments
tenements   jobs   churches
prisons   bottles   and
left untouched for decades

no rights, no refuge, no advocates,
we are borders in search
of countries, limiting ourselves,
fencing ourselves in -
products of too much production

we admire the view
beyond firing squads &
burger joint fast food wrappers,

we breath in smog, manifestos, shame,
and billboards before
a single nod -

fetch the luggage,
they do not want us here.

MAYBE

maybe i'm dying
or maybe this is life
coloring outside the lines -

dripping green into red, ranging over darkened thick borders
until everything is a concave fantasy folding inwards on itself
these placemats of history trace back our ancestry
to the original thief who ran away with all the forever & amen.

flying closer to the sun:
my crayons are melting, so i work fast -
pushing hues and shades around on pulp
that keeps getting stuck in my teeth,
stuck in my mind,
stuck in my throat -
faux utopia further away with every stroke.

maybe i'm dying
or maybe this is life
coloring outside the lines -

i've got a crate full of permanent markers,
the good ones with the metal barrels that give off fumes
making the room spin in that pleasant way,
the good ones that make bullshit tolerable.

my markers are the colors of the rainbow -
purple for the hearts i've won living in crossfire,
blue for the blood that's been spilled by my benefactors,
yellow for the stripe down my back as i've froze,
orange for all the things that rhyme with nothing else,
and red for the heart that breaks in on itself.

maybe i'm dying
or maybe this is life
coloring outside the lines?

THIS

brothers!
brothers please!

in times of war, horses are spared
for air, which is cut by rockets
moving above while messages travel
below.
       somewhere between, the roses
are minding sunshine & rain, aware
but uncaring, knowing their time
(fleeting as it is) will be met
without
       tears as we tear each other
apart, too busy for all that transpires
in our view - unaware of anything
but mistaken self-importance
internally
       a mystery while sunflowers
sway in the breeze, whispering:

this is a house of peace!
this is a house of peace!
this is a house of peace!

I GO TO SEEK
A GREAT PERHAPS:

dreams will be dreams &
feathers fall (as always)
as leaded tears
down to melt.

do you know names?
of unfavorable winds
       directions unknown
       faceless marble bumps
planted row on row
       do you know?

names like dust:
forgetful of origins
singlemindedly blown into cracks -
a hundred years within each
speck, greeted
by a perhaps

we hope to see
again.

DIONYSUS

his meditation was
slowly peeling the soppy-wet
labels from his bottles
with fingernail
chewed down to the quick -

a bartsool buddha
with none of the serenity,
only a bald head
& bulk.

"every damn fool thing
            you do in this life
you pay for," he said

the previous drinks
hung on his breath,
this time another time
when it was probably
time to quit -

but time is the only thing
left to kill
after the heart goes.

CURRENCY

the exit sign is the same:
stiff white hospital sheets &
mechanical chirps a final lullabye.
gone are all the bought goods
of a lifetime's conquest:

>   cars, whiskey, wine, women,
>   friends, politicians, & favors

vanished.

>   and only this thought remains:
>   money can't buy life.

when that tab comes due, no credit
is good enough - no bullion or jewels,
no off-shore accounts or secretive stash -
only the currency we brought
into this world:

ourselves.

all else is speculation that evaporates
when markets crash
at the closing bell.

money buys most anything
except the most valued commodity
of all - the ticking of clocks
& breath.

SHE SPOKE

i must go in, for the fog is rising -
these days have been numbered,
stacked, & collated for ambivalent consumption

the dreariness of every day
drowned in our own dysfunctional
delusion of stardom - fame in microcosm

the fog rises a little further,
pushing in at the boundaries,
waiting for nothing & taking everything

i must go in, for the fog is rising -
forgotten on the pile
is dignity and simple moments

replaced by a million snapshots
of nothing; a thousand somethings
that represent a vacuous hole

and into that hole, nothing but fog -
nothing but the fog rises, and she must go
or be taken along regardless.

THE BIG LIE

words duller than baseballs,
lines hurtling off rails -

i'm just tired

this is the lie
told hundreds of times
as an unconcerned world
spins, souls shed weight,
& bodies are recycled
to dust

and other writers
are left
to explain
it all.

MANTRA

there is but one reliance

>paper roses & burning tigers,
>unambitious lovers who become dust
>and circuitous deceit

there is but one reliance

>the radio spilling lies into my ears
>news stories that never end soon enough
>and unending commercial breaks

there is but one reliance

>charles mingus at midnight
>becoming another becoming
>and oh lord oh lord oh lord

there is but one reliance

>to thine own self be true
>wine stains where there should be blood
>and ice cubes where eyes should be

there is but one reliance

>but i have given it over to others
>to decipher and decide
>and kept myself to myself

there is but one reliance.

INSOMNIA REQUIEM

my eyes have seen too much
to ever remember

they are tired and weary of days
as cats staring out at the sun from shade

we are beggars, this is true
choosers of a great, faceless nothing

shapes, colors, and motion
trapped inside of me

nowhere to go, racing in circles
as i lie awake; a hostage,

the circus from hell plays out
behind my eyelids each night

films without sound or plot, misfits
of nature and abominations await

sleep refuses to come
visions refuse to go

a desert of stars stretches out
across the sheets into darkness

are these hallucinations?
or ghosts of my own sins?

it's all so wonderfully twisted and mad,
frightening and beautiful between blinks

performing mathematics moment by moment
calculating the sleep lost

logic disappears and my cupped hand rises,
for alms - for one moment of peace.

SUSTAIN

it's amazing:
the conductivity of phosphor bronze
through callouses won with hard labor,
the electricity of a note buzzing inside skull
like a fork jammed in an electrical socket
& the whole of the moon is there
on the other side trying to get through.

one note
changes the room's temperature,
a chord brings heads around from other
dimensions, eyes squint through haze,
ears cough out smoke - curiosity
abandons the cat to its own devices
& wonders what the hell is happening here?

conjuring & cajoling,
the cacophony comes
from some other place, bounces around
corners, then returns there without
ever purchasing a ticket - a roundtrip
without leaving, traces of nothing
scattered for all to see.

doctor, if i put this here guitar down now,
i ain't never gonna wake up.

for Bill

COOL WATERS

let us cross
the river
& rest

      under the shade
      of the trees -

forsaking
winter, fall,
spring & summer

      hooded garments
      sundresses & these:

beyond waters
sweet, cool,
& clear

      shines some kind
      of light that leaves

holes inside
& out of all
it beholds,

      never looking down
      at what it sees.

daring death
the first
mistake

      and the last: life
      on the trapeze.

ONE LAST DRINK, PLEASE

with each sip, my thirst grows
and i think
this shouldn't be
but yet it is
and so i dive deeper,
trying to find shadows
of myself long exiled
to the dark corners of memory.

with each gulp, my regret grows
and i think
this is how it must be:
a daring descent into the center,
but of what?
of myself or the numbness of you?

with each swallow, this poison
tastes a little bit sweeter
and i understand how hemlock
could be a cocktail
worthy of consideration,
your eyes the last thing i'll ever see
before moving into some other phase.

with each moment,
this time grows shorter
and dimmer, but you
become more brilliant,
which is why
i must go.

BACK IN NO TIME

she said she was going for cigarettes
and it was six months
before i remembered
she didn't smoke.

said she'd be back in no time
and it was ages
before i understood
what she really meant.

there's no time like the present
and there's no present like time,
only this purgatory of now
where i am
and she ain't.

said she was going for a walk
and it was a thousand steps
afterwards when
her ghost crossed the horizon.

said she's be back in no time
and today, it hit me
that there's no going back -
not home or any
where.

the space we leave in others
is the space we carry with us,
and i realized
she must be more space
than anything else.

so i went back
to staring at the clock.

YOU BE GOOD.
SEE YOU TOMORROW.
I LOVE YOU.

walking in miniature,

mirror image full of dreams -

delicate smile gleaming

diamond of hope

staring straight through souls,

with perfect eyes.

INDEX OF QUOTES

ONE

9 - "We are running on line north and south." - *Amelia Earhart, aviator*

10 - "I'm going away tonight." - *James Brown, singer & Godfather of Soul*

11 - "I hope so." - *Andrew Carnegie, American industrialist & philanthropist*

12 - "Don't lift me." - *Robert Kennedy, United States Attorney General*

14 - "I won't be long." - *Gabe MacConnell, friend*

15 - "I'm the problem." - *David A. Burke, skyjacker*

16 - "Suppose, suppose." - *Wyatt Earp, lawman*

18 - "Please don't let me fall." - *Mary Surratt, Lincoln assassination conspirator*

19 - "I expected it to happen." - *Pino Puglisi, Roman Catholic priest*

20 - "How can I ever forget them." - *Charles M. Shulz, cartoonist*

22 - "Bourbon... codeine..." - *Talulah Bankhead, American actress*

23 - "Pardon me. I didn't do it on purpose." - *Marie Antoinette, Queen of France*

24 - "Surprise me." - *Bob Hope, comedian & entertainer*

25 - "I can't breath." - *Eric Garner, murdered by the NYPD*

26 - "Now comes the mystery." - *Henry Ward Beecher, American minister*

26 - "Don't disturb my circles!" - *Archimedes, Greek mathematician*

27 - "Don't worry... it's not loaded." - *Terry Kath, musician & founding member of the band Chicago*

28 - "You will not find me alive at sunrise." - *Nostradamus, French astrologer*

35 - "Give me coffee, I'm going to write." - *Olavo Bilac, Brazilian poet*

36 - "Nothing soothes pain like human touch." - *Bobby Fischer, chess grandmaster*

37 - "For hearing, we need a language." - *M.N. Vijayan, Indian columnist*

38 - "Have I played the part well? Then applaud me as I exit." - *Augustus Caesar, Roman emporer*

40 - "I'll sleep well tonight." - *Henry Ford, American industrialist*

41 - "I can hear the music all around me." - *Dudley Moore, actor*

42 - "Good night my kitten." - *Ernest Hemingway, novelist & journalist*

44 - "So here it is." - *Cleopatra, last ruler of the Ptolemaic Kingdom of Egypt*

45 - "I feel pain here." - *Charles de Gaulle, President of France*

47 - "Never drive at night." - *Joseph Lucas, lamp manufacturer*

49 - "Love one another." - *William Henry Seward, United States Secretary of State*

50 - "It's very beautiful out there." - *Thomas Edison, inventor*

52 - "Why is this taking so long?" - *David Goodall, botanist*

53 - "Am I dying, or is this my birthday?" - *Lady Nancy Astor, British politician*

54 - "Hold the cross high so that I may see it through the flames." - *Joan of Arc, heroine of France & saint*

55 - "Don't be in such a hurry." - *Billie Holliday, singer*

56 - "Go away, I'm all right." - *H.G. Wells, writer*

57 - "You are wonderful." - *Sir Arthur Conan Doyle, writer*

59 - "Yes, but not too much." - *Gerrit Achterberg, Dutch poet*

61 - "I am a broken piece of machinery. When the machine is broken... I am ready." - *Woodrow Wilson, 28th U.S. President*

THREE

65 - "Last words are for fools who haven't said enough." - *Karl Marx, philosopher*

66 - "Does my face look strange?" - *Robert Louis Stevenson, writer*

67 - "I know not what tomorrow will bring." - *Fernando Pessosa, Portugese poet*

69 - "So here it is." - *Cleopatra, last ruler of the Ptolemaic Kingdom of Egypt*

71 - "I wish I could go with you." - *Walt Kelly, American animator*

72 - "Fetch the luggage, they do not want us here." - *Simon Bolivar, President of Gran Colombia*

74 - "Maybe I'm dying." - *Jim Henson, puppeteer & filmmaker*

76 - "Brothers! Brothers, please! This is a house of peace!" - *Malcolm X, American minister & activist*

77 - "I go to seek a great perhaps." - *Francois Rabelais, French writer*

78 - "Every damn fool thing you do in this life you pay for." - *Edit Piaf, singer*

79 - "Money can't buy life." - *Bob Marley, Jamaican singer-songwriter*

80 - "I must go in, for the fog is rising." - *Emily Dickinson, American poet*

81 - "I'm just tired." - *Chris Cornell, musician & lead singer of Soundgarden*

82 - "There is but one reliance." - *Martin Van Buren, 8th U.S. President*

83 - "We are beggars, this is true." - *Martin Luther, German professor of theology*

85 - "Doctor, if I put this here guitar down now, I ain't never gonna wake up." - *Leadbelly, American singer & blues pioneer*

86 - "Let us cross the river and rest under the shade of the trees."
- General Thomas "Stonewall" Jackson, Confederate general

87 - "One last drink, please." *- Jack Daniel, distiller*

88 - "Back in no time." *- William S. Burroughs, American writer*

90 - "You be good. See you tomorrow. I love you." *- Alex, African Grey Parrot*

ABOUT THE AUTHOR

Todd Regoulinsky is a husband, father, writer, musician, and several other things who grew up living in New Hampshire before settling into Maine over eighteen years ago. He is a graduate of the University of New Hampshire and has held many jobs that have very little to do with the degree he attained there, but it was fun nonetheless. He published a collection of his poems called *Odd Bits Of Broken Things* in 2008.

He can be found online at www.toddregoulinsky.com.